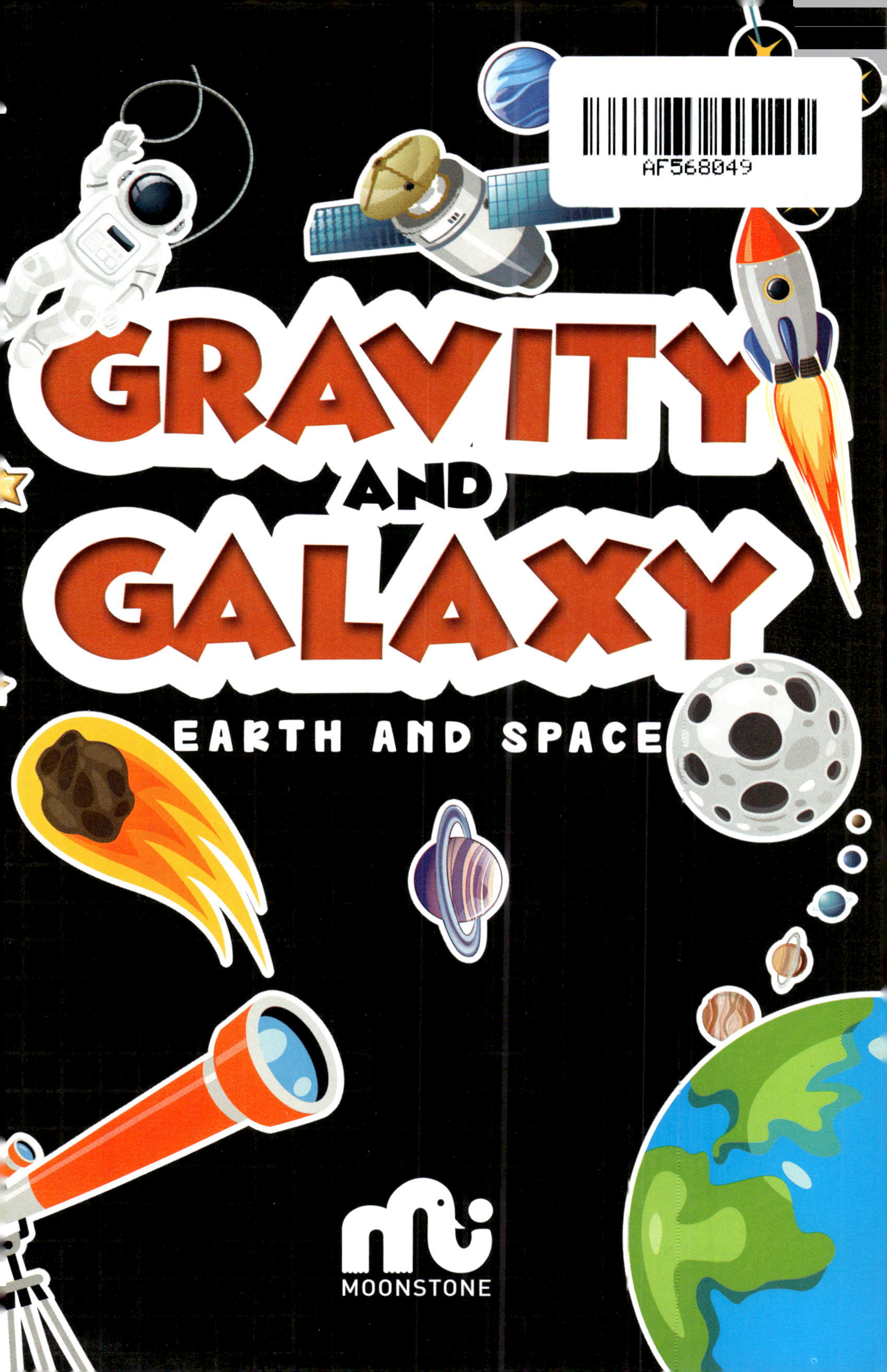
GRAVITY AND GALAXY
EARTH AND SPACE
MOONSTONE

Published in Moonstone
by Rupa Publications India Pvt. Ltd 2024
7/16, Ansari Road, Daryaganj
New Delhi 110002

Sales centres:
Bengaluru Chennai
Hyderabad Jaipur Kathmandu
Kolkata Mumbai Prayagraj

P-ISBN: 978-93-5702-390-0
E-ISBN: 978-93-5702-444-0

First impression 2024

10 9 8 7 6 5 4 3 2 1

Printed in India

CONTENTS

EARTH

CONTENTS

SPACE

EARTH AND SPACE
EARTH

Introduction

Earth is one of the eight planets in the solar system. It revolves around the sun at an average speed of 30 kilometres (about 18.5 miles) per second in an elliptical orbit. Earth is the only planet in the solar system that is known to support life. Oxygen, water, and the right temperature are necessary for life to exist. Earth has all of these favourable conditions, which make life possible.

Earth is the third planet from the Sun in the solar system. It is made up of rocks and metals. There are hot, molten rocks inside the earth's core and hard rocks on the surface or the crust of the earth. All of the continents are formed by the crust. The continents are separated by oceans and seas.

The Planet

Earth is the fifth-largest planet in the solar system. It lies 149.28 million kilometres (about 93 million miles) away from the sun. It has one natural satellite—the moon, which revolves around it.

Earth's Formation

Earth was formed 4.6 billion years ago. At that time, the solar system was a cloud of gas and dust. As time passed, the sun and planets were created out of that cloud of gas and dust. In the beginning, the earth was a red, hot ball of molten rocks. After many years, the earth cooled, and water vapour in the air formed oceans.

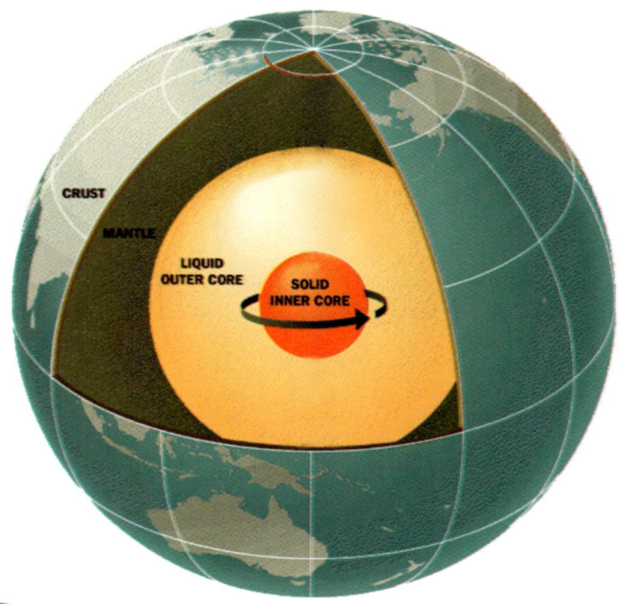

Layers

The interior of the earth is made up of three different layers. The first layer is the crust. It is made of soil, clay and fine rocks. The second layer is the mantle. It is made of solid, hot rocks. The core lies at the centre of the earth. It is made of molten nickel and iron.

Atmosphere

Earth is surrounded by a layer of gases called the atmosphere. The atmosphere protects the earth from the harmful radiation of the sun. It is made up of five layers. The atmosphere is 600 kilometres (about 375 miles) thick, and has no definite end point. It gradually becomes thinner until it merges into space.

- Earth's moon is one-quarter the size of the earth.
- Earth is the only planet in the solar system to have water in all three states—solid, liquid and gas.

How old is the Earth?

Rocks and Minerals

Rocks are hard and solid natural materials that can be found all over the earth, including in the polar regions and beneath the oceans. Rocks have been present on earth for millions of years. Minerals are crystals, which make up rocks. One or more minerals combine to make different kinds of rock.

Gemstones

Gemstones are expensive minerals that are used to make jewelry. Minerals are cut and polished to make gemstones. Topaz, diamond, ruby and emerald are a few examples of gemstones.

Rock Cycle

Rocks can change into other rocks or be recycled into new rocks. When a volcano erupts, molten rock or magma flows out as lava from inside the earth. As the lava cools, it forms igneous rocks. Weathering and erosion turn igneous rocks into sand and sediments. Sand reaches rivers and oceans to form many layers. These layers form sedimentary rocks. The movement of the earth's plates produces heat and melts the sedimentary rocks to form metamorphic rocks. Over time, the metamorphic rocks again form magma.

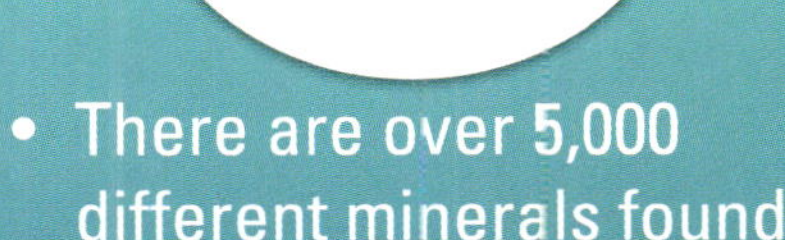

- There are over 5,000 different minerals found in the earth's crust.
- Manufactured materials like steel, bronze and plastic are not minerals.
- 24 karat gold means pure gold; 12 karat means half gold and half copper or another metal.

Fossils

Fossils are the remains of prehistoric animals and plants that are preserved under the earth's surface. The word "fossil" comes from the Latin word *fossilis*, which means "having been dug up." Fossils take millions of years to form.

Diamond is a gemstone. (True or False)

Climate

Climate is the average weather of a place, usually over a period of 30 years. The weather in any place keeps changing, but its climate remains the same. The climate of any region depends on its altitude and location on the globe, its distance from the sea, and the average atmospheric temperature and pressure.

Seasons

The seasons are caused by the earth's revolution around the sun and the tilt of its axis. It takes Earth 365 days to complete one revolution around the sun. During summer, the 23.5-degree tilt of the earth's axis makes the northern hemisphere lean towards the sun, which results in more daylight hours and more concentrated sunlight. During winter, the northern hemisphere leans away from the sun.

Facts

- A winter on Uranus lasts for 21 years!
- Average winter temperature drops to -34° C (-30° F) in the Arctic.
- The branch of meteorology which studies clouds is called nephology.

Day and Night

Day and night occur because of the earth's rotation. The earth rotates on an imaginary axis or central rod. Each rotation of the earth takes 24 hours to complete. During its rotation, the part of the earth that receives sunlight experiences days. The part of the earth away from the sun remains dark and experiences night.

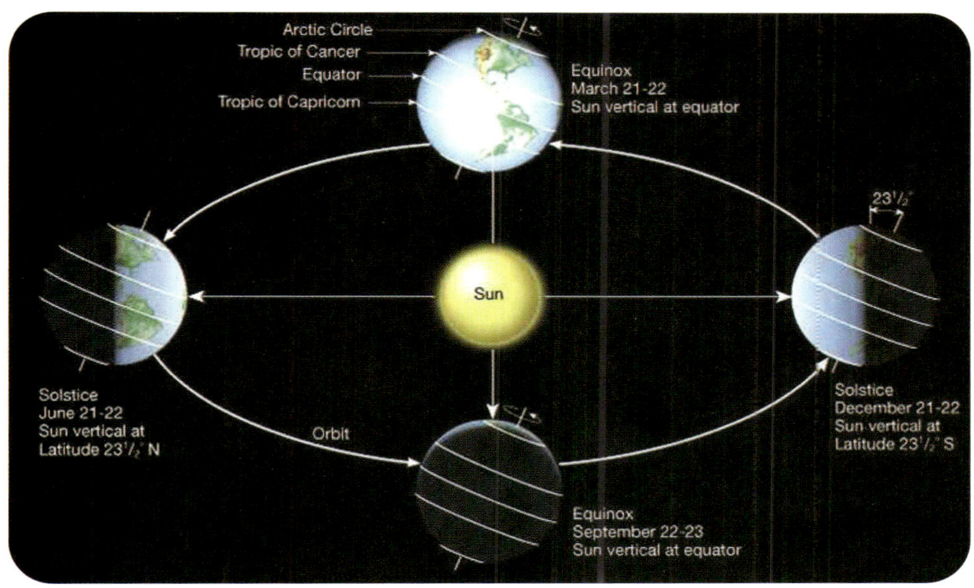

Temperature Difference

Earth is an irregularly shaped ellipsoid, which means the sun's rays hit different areas at different angles. Along the equator, the sun's rays strike the earth's surface directly. Therefore, areas near the equator are the hottest. As we move away from the equator, the sun's rays become slanted, which makes these places colder.

 **How much time does the earth take to complete one revolution?**

Weather

Weather is the condition of the earth's atmosphere at any given time and place. All changes in weather occur in the lower atmosphere of the earth. Weather changes because of many factors, like wind, temperature, humidity and sky conditions.

Floods

Floods are caused when water rises above its surrounding land. Water can rise because of heavy rainfall over a long period of time or when glacial ice or mountain snow melts. Some floods also occur when there is a heavy amount of rainfall over a short period of time. Floods can destroy homes and crops. They can even wash away fertile soil from farmlands, making them barren.

Clouds

Clouds are groups of very tiny water droplets or ice crystals. When these small droplets move along with the wind, different types of clouds are formed. Generally, there are three types of clouds: cirrus, or high clouds; alto, or middle clouds; and stratus, or low clouds.

Hurricanes

Hurricanes are violent storms. They rotate around an "eye." Hurricanes are dangerous and can cause great destruction because they are accompanied by rain, thunder, and lightning. Hurricanes move at high speeds. Sometimes their speed reaches up to 345 kilometres (215 miles) per hour.

- About 75 percent of the world's tornadoes occur in the United States.
- Clouds are white because they reflect the light of the sun. Light is made up of all the colours of the rainbow. When you add these colours together, you get a white colour.

What are hurricanes?

Continents

Continents are large, continuous landmasses on the earth's crust. They cover 29 percent of the earth's surface. Continents are separated by water. There are seven continents on Earth. Asia is the largest, and Australia is the smallest continent.

Continental Drift Theory

The Continental Drift Theory was developed by Alfred Wegener, a German meteorologist, in 1912. The theory states that 225 million years ago, all of the earth's landmass was merged into a single supercontinent. Later, as the earth's plates moved, pieces of land drifted away from each other, forming new continents. The theory goes on to explain that the continents are still drifting apart.

Africa

Africa is the world's second-largest continent. It covers about 20 percent of the world's area, after Asia. Africa has the highest number of countries. There are 54 countries in Africa. The world's longest river, the Nile, and the largest desert, the Sahara, are in Africa.

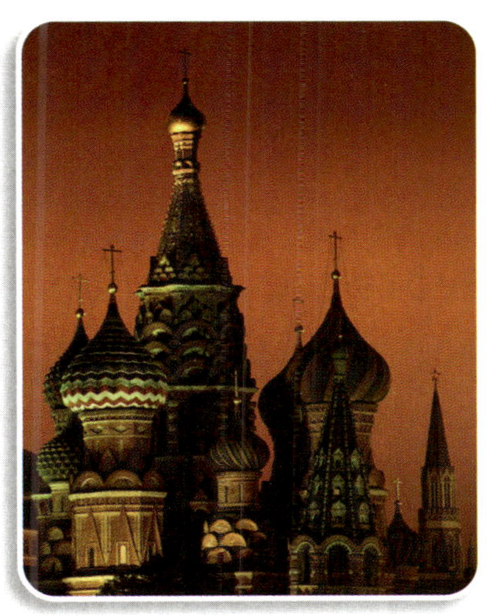

Asia

Asia is the world's most populous continent. Sixty percent of the world's population lives in Asia. Asia has 48 countries covering 30 percent of the earth's total land area. Russia, the world's biggest country, is a part of Asia.

Antarctica

Antarctica is one of the seven continents. It lies on the southernmost portion of the earth. It is also the coldest region on Earth. The only humans who live in Antarctica are scientists, who live in specially built bases. There are more than 1,100 species inhabiting the ice continent, like penguins, seals, orcas, etc.

Facts

- The Ural Mountains separate the two continents of Asia and Europe.
- There are no deserts in Europe.
- Antarctica is the only continent that does not have any countries.
- Turkey is part of both Europe and Asia.

 **How many continents are there in the world?**

Water

Water is the source of all life. It is important for all living beings. Glaciers, rivers, lakes and oceans are sources of water. About 97 percent of the earth's water is stored in the oceans.

Water Cycle

The sun heats up the ocean water, which evaporates to form water vapour. This water vapour makes the air moist. Moist air cools down and forms tiny droplets of water, which form clouds. When these water droplets in clouds become heavy, they fall as rain or snow. This recycling of water between the earth and the atmosphere is known as the water cycle.

Facts

- The Pacific Ocean is twice as large as the Atlantic Ocean.
- The Great Lakes, on the Canada–United States border, make up the largest group of freshwater lakes in the world.
- The world's second-largest river, the Amazon River, stores 20 percent of the world's total freshwater.

Rivers

Rivers are large freshwater streams. They flow for long distances. They are formed by melting snow, glaciers, or rainfall. At their points of origin, rivers are narrow, but on their downhill journey, they merge with other streams or rivers to form large rivers. Rivers end up in lakes, oceans, bays, seas or other large water bodies.

Lakes

Lakes are freshwater bodies. Water in lakes is generally calmer than in the oceans and seas. Some lakes are large, while others are small. Lakes are usually deep. Lake Baikal in Russia is the deepest lake in the world.

? **Rivers are ________ bodies.**

Oceans And Seas

Oceans and seas are large saltwater bodies. They cover more than 70 percent of the surface of the earth. They are home to millions of living organisms. There are five world oceans and many seas on earth.

Seas, Gulfs and Estuaries

Seas are much smaller than oceans. Gulfs and estuaries are coastal water bodies that are surrounded by land. Gulfs are quieter than open oceans as the surrounding land reduces winds and blocks the waves. Estuaries, on the other hand, are the water bodies where seawater mixes with the fresh water coming from the land.

Life in Oceans

From the sunlit layers to the deep, murky waters, oceans abound in various life forms. Ocean life can be classified into three groups: plankton, nekton, and benthos. All animals, from squids and scallops to the gigantic whales that can swim freely, belong to nektons. Plankton are plant-like organisms that float on the surface of water. Animals such as anemones, worms, crabs, flatfish, and hagfish that live near the ocean floor are known as benthos.

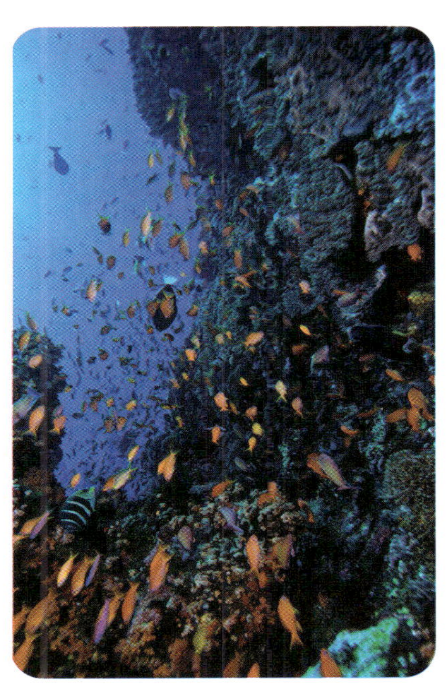

Largest and Smallest

The Pacific Ocean, Atlantic Ocean, Indian Ocean, Arctic Ocean, and Southern Ocean are the five oceans on earth. Of all the world's oceans, the Pacific Ocean is the largest and deepest. The Arctic Ocean is the smallest and shallowest ocean in the world.

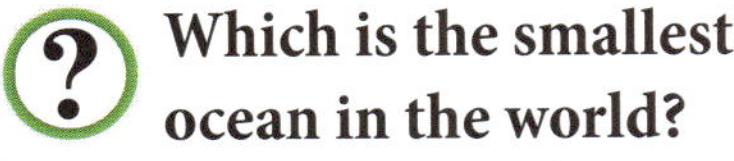

- There are about 20,000 kinds of fish living in the oceans.
- The Southern Ocean is also called the Antarctic Ocean as it surrounds the continent of Antarctica.
- The Arctic Ocean remains semi-frozen all year and is completely surrounded by land.

Mountains

Mountains are high landforms on the earth's surface. They are higher than their surroundings. Mountains are surrounded by rivers, valleys or plains. Mountains are found everywhere on the earth, even below the oceans.

Highest Mountain Peak

Mount Everest is the highest mountain peak in the world. This 8,850-metre (about 29,035 feet) high mountain is a part of the Himalayan Mountain Range, which spans the border of Nepal and Tibet. Mount Everest is about 60 million years old.

Facts

- Tibet, India, and Nepal are visible from Mount Everest.
- The Himalayas is home to the world's 30 highest mountain peaks.
- The length of the Andes Mountain Range is more than 7,000 kilometres (4,350 miles).

How are mountains formed?

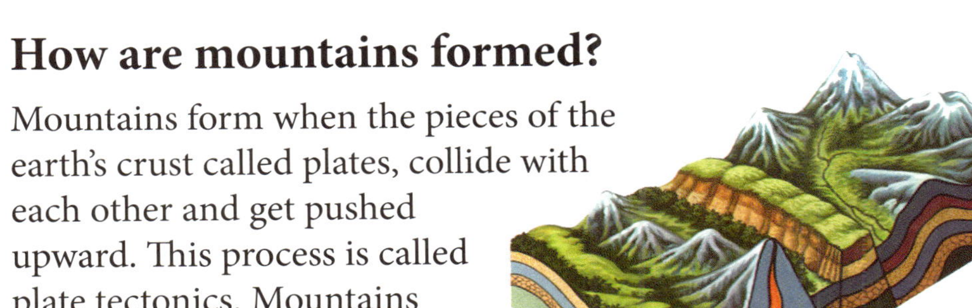

Mountains form when the pieces of the earth's crust called plates, collide with each other and get pushed upward. This process is called plate tectonics. Mountains have sloping sides and ridges with sharp or round ends.

Mauna Kea

Mauna Kea or "White Mountain," is an inactive volcano located on the island of Hawaii in the Pacific Ocean. Mauna Kea is more than 10,000 meters (32,808 feet) tall when measured from its base at the bottom of the Pacific Ocean. However, it rises only 4,200 meters (about 13,779 feet) above the sea level.

Mountain Ranges

Mountain ranges are a series of mountains that are close to each other. The Andes Mountain Range in South America is the longest mountain range in the world. The Himalayan Mountain Range contains the world's highest mountains.

Name the highest mountain in the world.

Earthquakes and Volcanoes

Earthquakes and volcanoes are natural disasters. Earthquakes are sudden movements or slipping of the surface of the earth. Volcanoes are openings in the earth's crust through which gases, hot steam and lava erupts. Earthquakes can destroy buildings and harm lives, while volcanoes can cause ash to fall, emit poisonous gases, and cause landslides.

What causes an earthquake?

The earth's surface is made of many large plates, which continuously move against each other and create stress. This stress and pressure create vibrations and can cause earthquakes.

Types of Volcanoes

Volcanoes may exist in any one of the three states—active, dormant or extinct. Active volcanoes erupt continuously. There are more than 1500 active volcanoes. Dormant volcanoes are the ones that have not erupted in the recent past while extinct volcanoes are dead. Volcanoes that are not expected to show any volcanic eruption in future are called inactive volcanoes.

Ring of Fire

The Ring of Fire is an area where earthquakes and volcanoes occur regularly. It is about 40,000 kilometres (about 24,855 miles) of horseshoe-shaped area that encircles the Pacific Ocean. The Ring of Fire contains 75 percent of the world's active and dormant volcanoes.

Where is Ring of Fire located?

- There are more than 1500 active volcanoes in the world.
- Moonquakes occur on the moon, just like earthquakes occur on earth.
- Mauna Loa, in Hawaii is the world's biggest volcano.

Soil

Soil makes up the outermost layer of the earth, and covers a quarter of its surface. It is made up of rock particles, sand, clay, air, water, and dead plant and animal matter. Soil can be brown, red, grey, or black in colour.

Formation of soil

It takes hundreds of years to form an inch of soil. Soil is formed from materials like rock particles, dead plants, animal remains, etc. Dead plants and animal remains are broken down into smaller components by microorganisms, whereas rocks are broken down into smaller particles by the action of wind, water, and rain.

Hub of life

Soil is an ecosystem where hundreds and thousands of diverse living organisms live and interact with each other. Soil is the source of different types of food and nutrients for these organisms. From the tiniest microorganisms like bacteria to medium-sized insects and spiders to larger burrowing animals such as rabbits all thrive in soil.

Types of soil

Sand, sand, clay, and loam are common types of soil. Sand is composed of larger rock particles than sand, whereas clay has very fine rock particles. All three soils have poor water drainage. On the other hand, loam is a mixture of sand, silt, clay, and dead and decayed plant and animal remains. This soil drains water perfectly and is good for plants.

- The outermost layer of soil is called topsoil.
- It takes about 500 years to form one to two centimeters of topsoil.
- Only about 11 percent of Earth's land surface is suitable for farming.

What is the outermost layer of soil called?

Biomes and Ecosystems

Biomes are a group of ecosystems that are marked by specific geographic and climatic conditions. They represent a large unit of the environment that has a vast store of biodiversity. The main kinds of biomes are grasslands, forests, tundra, deserts, and aquatic.

What is an Ecosystem?

An ecosystem is about the interaction of different living organisms with each other and their environment. All living beings depend on each other for growth and survival. An ecosystem can be as small as a tree or as large as the entire forest.

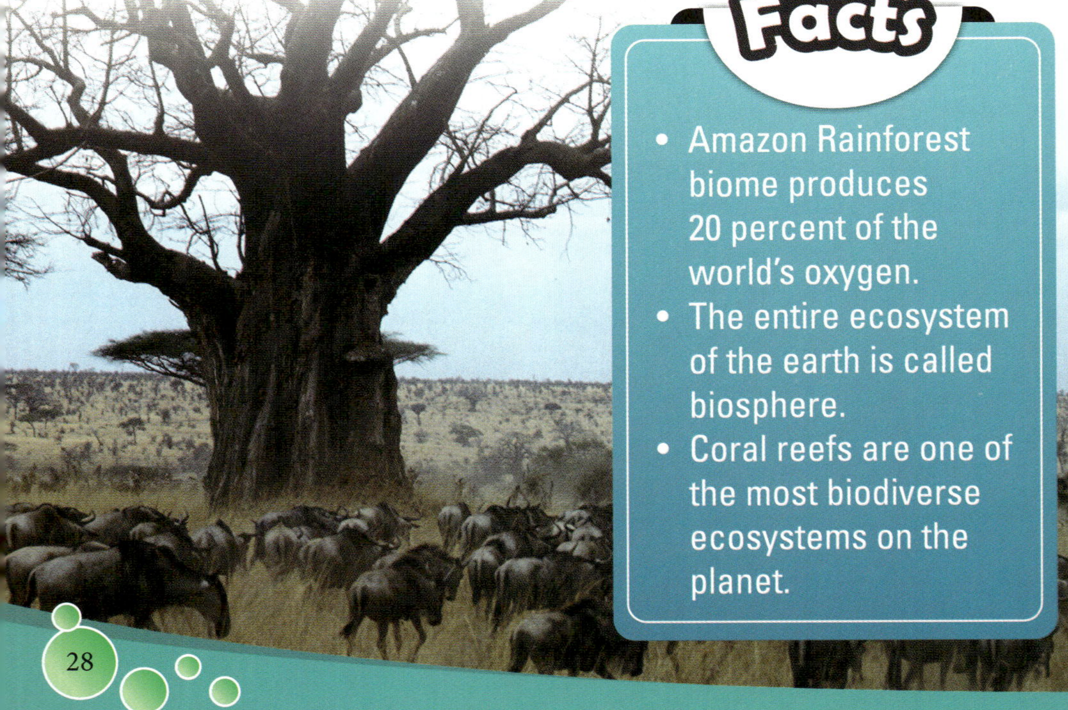

Facts

- Amazon Rainforest biome produces 20 percent of the world's oxygen.
- The entire ecosystem of the earth is called biosphere.
- Coral reefs are one of the most biodiverse ecosystems on the planet.

Structure of an Ecosystem

An ecosystem is made up of producers, consumers, decomposers and non-living things such as air, water, soil, etc. Producers are those living organisms that can make their own food such as plants. Consumers are those living organisms that cannot produce their own food and feed on other living organisms. On the other hand, decomposers are microorganisms such as bacteria that break down the dead and decayed remains of plants and animals.

Ecological Cycles

Carbon, nitrogen and water are essential nutrients that are needed for life on earth. These nutrients keep circulating from the atmosphere to the living organisms and then back to the atmosphere. This movement of carbon, water and nitrogen in an ecosystem is known as the ecological cycle.

Is grassland a biome?

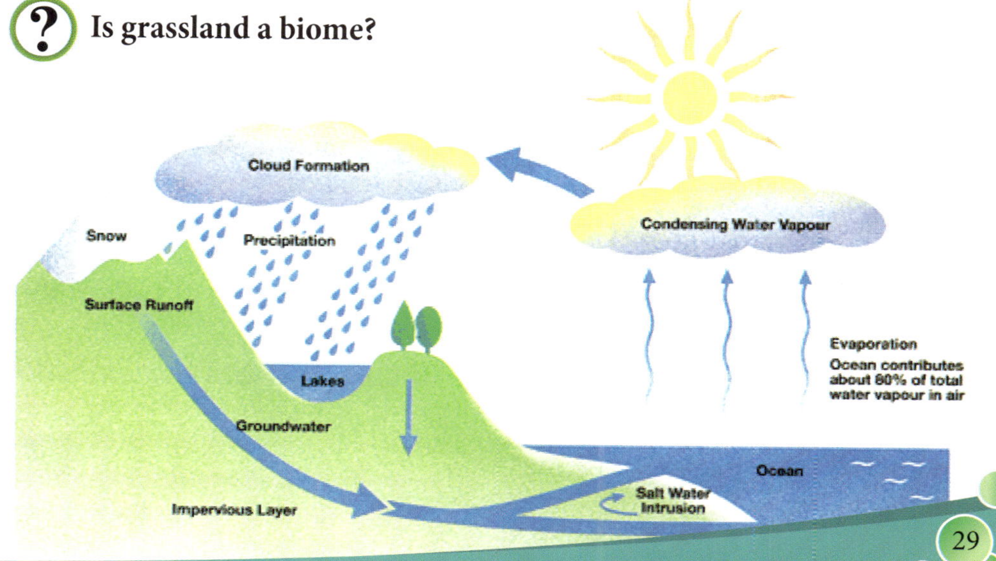

Forests

Forests are large and dense areas with trees, plants, animals and birds. Around 30 percent of the earth's land is covered with forests. Forests are found all over the world.

Rainforests

Rainforests are very dense, warm and wet forests. Heavy rainfall occurs here. Rainforests are home to rare species of plants, birds and animals. They cover less than 2 percent of the earth's total surface area. Rainforests are home to more than 50 percent of the earth's plants and animals.

What is a wildfire?

Wildfires are uncontrollable fires that occur in dry forests and grasslands. They can be caused by lightning, volcanic eruptions or heat waves. Wildfires spread quickly, igniting dry trees and other vegetation. Firefighters cut down trees to create open ground to stop wildfires.

Rainforest Layers

Rainforests are made of four layers—emergent, canopy, understory, and forest floor. The forest floor is hot and humid and receives only 2 percent sunlight. The understory receives a little sunlight, and plants grow up to 3.65 metres (about 12 feet). The canopy is a dense roof of trees where trees grow up to 45.72 metres (about 150 feet) in height. The canopy is crossed by the trees of the emergent layer. The trees of the emergent layer rise up to 61 metres (about 200 feet); however, their numbers are low.

- Four out of five wildfires are caused by humans.
- Only one-fifth of the earth's original forests are left.
- Tropical rainforests cover less than 3% of the planet but support more than half of all terrestrial animal species.

Forests cover about ________ of the surface of earth.

Deserts

Deserts are dry land areas that are either very hot or very cold. Cold deserts are found in the Polar Regions, while hot deserts are found in the rest of the world. Hot deserts receive very little rainfall and have high temperatures. Deserts cover more than one-fifth of the earth's land.

- The word "Sahara" in Arabic means "wilderness."
- The Atacama Desert of South America is the driest desert in the world.
- The most common animal found in the desert is the camel, which stores food in its hump in the form of fat.

Sahara

The Sahara Desert in northern Africa is the largest hot desert in the world. It is so large that it spreads across ten countries—Morocco, Algeria, Libya, Egypt, Niger, Chad and Sudan. The temperature of the Sahara Desert reaches up to 50°C (122°F) during the day.

Sand Dunes

Sand dunes are small hills or mounds of sand. They are formed in deserts when strong winds blow in a certain area. Winds with different speeds are responsible for making different types of sand dunes. Sand dunes found in the Sahara Desert can reach a height of up to 300 metres (about 984 feet).

Oasis

Oases are small vegetated areas in deserts that are formed by one or more springs trapped between rocks under the desert floor. Palm trees can be found near oases, which provide shade for animals and travellers.

________ is the largest hot desert in the world.

Grasslands

Grasslands are large, and flat open areas covered with grasses. They are generally found where not enough rainfall occurs. Most grasslands are found between forests and deserts. Grasslands cover about 25 percent of the earth's surface.

Prairies

Prairies are large and flat grasslands usually dominated by herbs and grasses. The North American prairie covers an area of about three million square kilometers. Many species of grasses grow here. Some of them can grow up to three metres (about 10 feet).

Facts

- Most of the dust bowls occurred between 1930 and 1936. This time period was known as the "dirty thirties."
- Grasslands are found everywhere except in Antarctica.
- Steppes have short grasses and prairies have tall grasses.

Dust Bowls

Dust bowls are dirt storms that look like huge clouds of dirt. They were very common in the Great Plain grasslands of North America during the 1930s. Due to a lack of rainfall, overgrazing and poor cultivation, the land became barren at that time. Thus, when strong winds blew, they formed large clouds of dust.

Slash and Burn

Slash and burn is a method to clear grasslands by putting them on fire. Forests and woodlands are burned to make fields ready for farming, livestock or grazing. The ash of burned trees improves the fertility of the land. It is an old method also used to control weeds.

What are dust bowls?

Polar Regions

Polar regions include the Arctic, located at the North Pole, and Antarctica, located at the South Pole. These regions remain covered with ice throughout the year. The Arctic is formed of only ice, while Antarctica is a landform covered with a very thick sheet of ice.

Icebergs

Icebergs are large broken pieces of ice that float in open water. They are mainly found in the Arctic Ocean. Some icebergs are just a few feet large while others can be many miles in size. Only 10 percent of the icebergs are visible; the rest remain hidden below the water.

Glaciers

Glaciers are large portions of slow-moving ice. Glaciers and ice sheets store about 80 percent of the earth's fresh water. They can be found on mountain terrains or they can cover large areas. Glaciers are found everywhere in the world except in Australia. Most of them are found in Antarctica, Alaska, and Greenland.

Facts

- Some icebergs weigh up to 200,000,000 tons.
- Glaciers cover around 10 percent of the earth's surface.
- Antarctica has six months of daylight and six months of darkness.

Arctic

The Arctic is the northernmost point of the earth. It includes parts of Europe, Russia, Alaska and Canada. The Arctic is mostly covered with ice throughout the year. However, it is warmer than Antarctica. About four million people live in the Arctic.

Do people live in the Arctic?

Natural Resources

Natural resources are resources supplied by nature. They include water, air, land, forests, fish, topsoil, oil, natural gas and minerals. Natural resources can be non-renewable, like coal, gas and petroleum products, or renewable like sunlight, wind, or water.

Recycling

Recycling is reusing old and used materials. It helps save the earth's natural resources. It also reduces pollution and saves energy. About 70 percent less energy is required to make recycled paper than what is needed to make paper from raw materials.

Renewable Sources of Energy

Renewable sources of energy are sources that can be replaced in a short time and can be used again and again. They include energy derived from wind, rain, sunlight, geothermal sources and oceans.

Fossil Fuels

Fossil fuels are mineral fuels formed from the remains of organic substances in the earth's crust. Oil, natural gas and coal are the major fossil fuels. The formation of fossil fuels took millions of years. Fossil fuel are non-renewable sources of energy, which will eventually run out.

Fossil fuels are ______ source of energy.

Facts

- In the United States, wind energy projects that are running in 30 states supply electricity to more than 2.0 million people.
- The world's top five crude oil-producing countries are the United States, Russia, Saudi Arabia, Brazil, and Iraq.

Saving the Earth

Earth is home to human beings, plants, and animals. The earth's atmosphere and water make life possible here. However, many human activities, like water pollution, the burning of fossil fuels, and deforestation, are causing widespread damage to the earth's environment. The time has now come for us to take action and save the earth from extinction.

Greenhouse Gases

Greenhouse gases trap the heat of the solar radiation in the atmosphere and keep the earth warm. Some greenhouse gases occur naturally, while others are emitted by human activities. Water vapour, carbon dioxide, methane, and hydrofluorocarbons are all greenhouse gases.

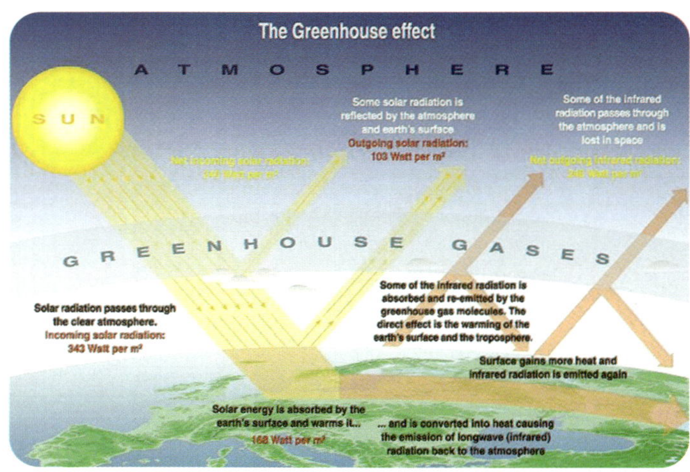

Global Warming

Global warming is the increase in the temperature of the earth that causes climate change. The warming of the earth causes changes in rainfall patterns, a rise in the sea level, and harmful effects on plants, animals, and humans.

Ozone Layer

The ozone layer is a thin protective layer of a natural colourless gas known as ozone. It protects the earth from the sun's ultraviolet radiation, which is harmful for humans. Ultraviolet radiation can cause diseases such as skin cancer, eye problems, or sunburn.

- A molecule of ozone is made up of three oxygen atoms.
- One recycled tin can save energy enough to power a television for three hours.
- Without greenhouse gases, the earth would be 30 degrees cooler and life would be impossible.

Carbon dioxide is not a greenhouse gas. (True or False)

Inhabitants of the Earth

Earth is the only planet that we know supports life. The earth's atmosphere, land and oceans support life on the earth. Plants, animals and human beings are major inhabitants of earth. Scientists believe that life originated on earth about 3.5 billion years ago.

Animals

Animals form one of the largest groups of living organisms, including insects, birds, reptiles, amphibians, fish and mammals. All animals have four important characteristics: they move, breathe, grow and reproduce. Ranging from the tiny mosquitoes to the gigantic blue whales, scientists believe that there may be around 30 million species of animals living on the earth.

Facts

- Plants release oxygen for us to breathe and they take in the carbon dioxide we release.
- Mammals give birth to live young ones, unlike other animals which lay eggs.
- Dinosaurs are extinct animals that lived on earth 65 million years ago.

Humans

Humans have a highly developed brain and mental capacity. Human intelligence and teamwork have made humans the most successful of all living beings. From hunter-gatherers to astronauts, humans have shown an amazing capacity to improve and innovate. Humans have used the earth's resources to create and build the modern world that we live in today.

Plants

Plants are a group of living things that include trees, flowers, shrubs, herbs, grasses and vines. They provide all living beings with oxygen, food and shelter. Plants are autotrophs. They manufacture their own food. About 500 million years ago, the first plants appeared on Earth. There are more than 390,000 known species of plants today.

? **Autotrophs make their own food. (True or False)**

Glossary

Astronaut: a person who is trained to travel in space

Collide: to strike violently against each other

Deforestation: the process of cutting down trees

Destruction: a process of destroying or damaging something

Dormant: inactive or in a state of rest

Equator: an imaginary line around the centre of the earth

Erosion: a process in which the surface of a rock gets damaged or weathered by water or wind

Erupt: to explode with a loud noise

Geothermal: related to the heat energy stored inside the earth

Gigantic: very big or huge

Innovate: to think of new ideas

Landform: a feature on the surface of the earth like a mountain

Landslide: a natural disaster in which large rocks and debris move down a slope

Merge: when something combines with another thing

Methane: a colourless and odourless gas

Metrology: a branch of science that studies the climate and weather of a place

Pollution: presence of harmful substances in air, water, and soil

Slash: to cut something using a sharp weapon

Species: a group of plants or animals with similar characteristics

Thunder: a loud noise that is heard in the sky during a storm or heavy rain

Tornado: a strong wind quickly going round in circles

Weathering: breaking down of rocks

Weed: an unwanted plant that grows easily almost everywhere

Answers

Page No. 9	4.6 billion years
Page No. 11	True
Page No. 13	365 days
Page No. 15	Violent storms
Page No. 17	Seven
Page No. 19	Freshwater
Page No. 21	Arctic Ocean
Page No. 23	Mount Everest
Page No. 25	Pacific Ocean
Page No. 27	Topsoil
Page No. 29	Yes
Page No. 31	30 percent
Page No. 33	Sahara Desert
Page No. 35	Dust storms
Page No. 37	Yes
Page No. 39	Non-renewable
Page No. 41	False
Page No. 43	True

EARTH AND SPACE
SPACE

Introduction

The universe is everything that exists. It includes the earth, everything on the earth, other planets, natural satellites, the Sun, and the billions of other stars and galaxies. It is believed that the universe was created billions of years ago in an explosion. This explosion scattered gas and matter to form galaxies, stars, and planets.

Since ancient times, the universe has been a mystery for humankind. Astronomers have recorded their observations for centuries. Many astronauts have been sent to explore planets and outer space with the help of space shuttles. These missions have greatly increased our knowledge about the universe.

Origin of the Universe

Around 14 billion years ago, the universe was born. In the beginning, it was a small fireball (even smaller than a pinhead) and hotter and denser than anything ever known. The small fireball exploded, and everything in the universe formed from this tiny particle. Since then, the universe has been growing and expanding.

What is the Universe made up of?

More than 95 percent of the vast span of the universe is composed of dark energy and dark matter, and the rest is made up of a mixture of gases. Hydrogen is the dominant gas. It accounts for almost 78 percent of the total composition of gases. Helium accounts for 20 percent, while various other gases make up the remaining two percent.

Big Bang

The Big Bang was a massive explosion that formed the universe about 14 billion years ago. Astronomers have not yet discovered any reason behind the explosion. However, the explosion was so powerful that the universe is still expanding at a constant speed.

Facts

- There are around 1022 to 1024 stars in the Universe.
- To fly as far as 1,000,000 kilometers (about 621,371 miles) in space, you would have to fly for six weeks on a jet without stopping.

End of the Universe

Astronomers believe that the universe might end in one of three ways. They believe that it might freeze and come to an end, or that all the galaxies will be swallowed by another black hole, or that the whole universe could slow down and then come to a halt.

Is the universe constantly expanding?

Galaxies

Galaxies are huge groups of stars, dust, and gas that are held together by gravity. Galaxies have billions of stars, and the universe has billions of galaxies. Scientists believe that more than 100 billion galaxies exist in the universe. Large galaxies have more than a trillion stars. The solar system is in a galaxy called the Milky Way.

Group of Galaxies

Some galaxies are found far from each other while others are found in pairs. The galaxies that are found in pairs orbit each other. Most galaxies are seen in groups known as clusters. A cluster can have a few dozen to several thousand galaxies.

Size of Galaxies

The universe is full of galaxies, and all of them are different sizes. Some of the galaxies are small and can hold less than a billion stars. Others are larger and can hold more than a trillion stars.

Spiral Galaxies

Spiral galaxies have a bulge in the center, which is surrounded by bright spiral arms. In spiral galaxies, new stars continuously form from dust and gas. The Milky Way is an example of a spiral galaxy.

Elliptical Galaxies

Elliptical galaxies are bright shining galaxies that are found endlessly throughout the universe. Very few new stars are formed in elliptical galaxies and most of them are made up of old stars.

Facts

- Andromeda Galaxy is a spiral galaxy and is visible to the naked eye from the northern hemisphere.
- In an elliptical galaxy, the light is brightest in the centre.

? **Milky Way is a _______ galaxy.**

Nebula

A nebula is a dense cloud of gas and dust in space. Stars begin their lives in a nebula. Nebulae have star-forming regions where gas, dust, and other materials clump together to form large masses to form stars, planets, and celestial objects. Nebulae are of three types: diffuse, supernova, and planetary nebulae.

Cat's Eye Nebula

The Cat's Eye Nebula is a planetary nebula. This nebula looks like a blue disc. It lies in the northern constellation of Draco. It is one of the most complex nebulae because it has knots, jets, and wiry arc-like features.

Diffuse Nebulae

Diffuse nebulae are wide clusters of dust and gas. Some diffuse nebulae contain enough dust and gases to form as many as 100,000 sun-like stars. They are found near very hot and bright stars or near cool stars. Diffuse nebulae are of three types: emission, reflection, and dark nebula.

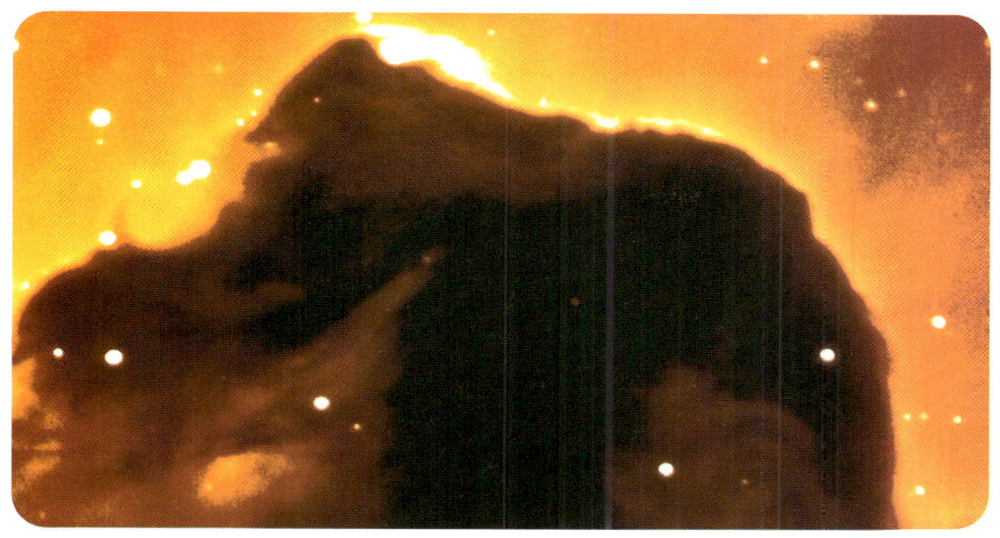

Great Nebula

The Great Nebula is an emission nebula in the constellation Orion. It is a huge cloud of dust and gas with a bright central area. This nebula, also known as the Orion Nebula, and is around 1,300 light years away from the earth.

Facts

- Nebula in Latin means cloud.
- Planetary nebulae are formed from dying stars.
- Sirius is over 20 times brighter and 2 times bigger than our sun.

In which constellation does the Cat's Eye Nebula lie?

Milky Way

The Milky Way is our home galaxy. It is a spiral galaxy with long arms that spin around in space. The Sun and most of the stars that we see at night are located in the arms of the Milky Way. There are more than 100 billion stars in the Milky Way.

Milky Way System

The dust and gas of the Milky Way are arranged into three components: the halo, the disc, and the centre. The halo is the spherical distribution of the galaxy with the oldest stars. The disc includes the sun, all the gases and dust, and most of its stars. The centre of the galaxy is called the nuclear bulge, or galactic centre.

How big is the Milky Way?

The Milky Way is over 100,000 light-years wide. It is so large that the Sun takes around 250 million years to complete an orbit around the Milky Way. The solar system is about 27,000 light years away from the centre of the Milky Way.

Facts

- It would take more than 6,340 years to count all the stars in the Milky Way.
- Scientists believe that the halo of the Milky Way contains globular clusters and dark matter.

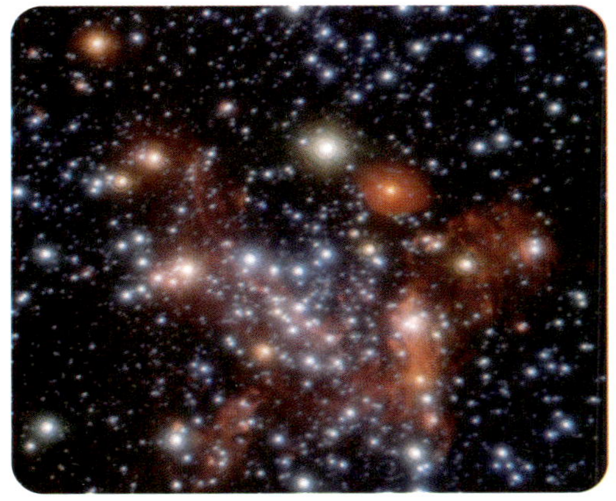

Inside the Milky Way

The Milky Way is a collection of stars, planets, asteroids, meteoroids and gas. The solar system lies within the Milky Way. The centre of the galaxy looks brighter because stars are more closely packed together there.

How wide is the Milky Way?

Solar System

The solar system includes the Sun and other celestial bodies. The sun lies at the centre of the solar system. Orbiting around the Sun are the major planets, their moons, dwarf planets, asteroids, comets, and meteoroids. The solar system was formed about 4.5 billion years ago.

How was the solar system formed?

Our solar system was formed from a large cloud of gas and dust known as the solar nebula. When the solar nebula began to collapse due to its own gravity, it formed a disc. The particles inside the disc collided and stuck together to form small objects. Some of them combined to form planets, while others formed moons, meteoroids, asteroids and comets.

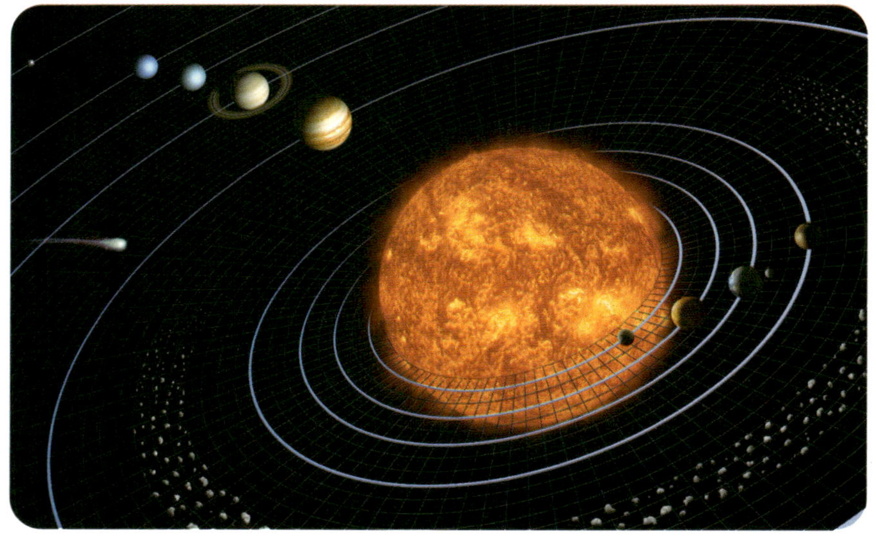

Dwarf Planets

Dwarf planets are celestial bodies that look like planets but are much smaller. Unlike planets, they do not have enough gravity to clear other objects from their orbits. Pluto is an example of a dwarf planet.

- Astronomers have discovered that more than 50 stars, like our Sun, have planets orbiting them.
- Mercury has the shortest orbit, while Neptune has the longest orbit among all planets.
- Many dwarf planets and asteroids also have moons.

Orbit

The sun is in the centre of the solar system, and all other objects orbit around it. Planets, meteoroids, and asteroids move in their respective orbits. However, all planets move around the sun in an anticlockwise direction.

What is Pluto?

Sun

The sun is a star. It is a huge burning ball of gas at the centre of the solar system. All planets (including the earth and celestial bodies in the solar system) orbit around the Sun. The Sun was formed about 4.6 billion years ago.

Sunspots

Sunspots are temporary dark spots on the surface of the sun. Sunspots appear dark because they are cooler than the surrounding regions. Sunspots are large enough to be seen with the naked eye. The largest sunspots have a diameter of 50,000 kilometres (about 31,069 miles).

Facts

- The burning of hydrogen with helium in the sun's core makes it shine brightly.
- Many sunspots are equal to the size of the earth.

How hot is the Sun?

The sun is very hot. The temperature at the centre or core is over 15 million degrees Celsius (27 million degrees Fahrenheit). The sun gives us light and warmth that are extremely important for life. Without the sun, the earth would be a dark and frozen planet.

How big is the Sun?

The Sun is a large star with an equatorial radius of 696,340 kilometres (about 440,000 miles). This is 109 times the diameter of the earth. The sun is so large that we could fit over one million earths inside it.

How old is the Sun?

Stars and Constellations

Stars are huge, brightly shining balls of hot gases in space. Stars give off light and other forms of energy. Stars are found in galaxies. About 75 percent of stars are found in pairs. A group of stars in a region of the night sky forms a constellation. Until now, 88 constellations have been spotted and named.

Names of Constellations

Constellations are named after different animals and mythological characters. For example, the constellation Leo is named after a lion and the constellation Orion is named after a Greek mythological character.

- All constellations can be viewed from the equator during the course of the year.
- On a starry night, we can see about 3,000 stars.

Star's Life Cycle

Stars are not permanent objects that twinkle in the sky. They are born, grow, age, and then die. The different phases of a star's life cycle are protostar, main sequence star, red giant, white dwarf, black dwarf, and supernova. A protostar is the earliest phase of a star. When the core of a protostar becomes very hot and dense, a main sequence star is formed. Main sequence stars burn hydrogen to form helium. They are the most luminous stars. Our Sun is a main sequence star. After burning hydrogen for millions of years, main sequence stars that are the size of our sun transform into red giants. Red giants lose their brightness and end up as white dwarfs. Stars that are bigger than our sun end their lives in a huge explosion known as a supernova.

? Some stars die in explosions known as ________.

Planets - Mercury and Venus

Our solar system has eight planets. All planets revolve around the sun, which is at the centre of the solar system. The planets Mercury and Venus are closest to the sun. They are called inner planets.

Mercury

Mercury is the first and nearest planet to the sun. Mercury moves faster than any other planet in the solar system. The planet moves at a speed of 48 kilometres (29.7 miles) per second and takes only 88 days to orbit around the sun.

Facts

- As Mercury has no atmosphere, the sky always looks black even during the day.
- Mercury spins on its axis very slowly and completes one spin in 58.6 days.

Mercury's surface

The surface of Mercury is covered with craters, cliffs, and valleys. There is no atmosphere or water on the planet. This is why the surface of the planet becomes very hot during the day and very cold during the night.

Venus

Venus is the second planet from the sun and closest to the earth. It is the brightest of all planets. Venus is covered with a sheet of thick clouds, which trap all the heat and make it very hot. It is even hotter than Mercury.

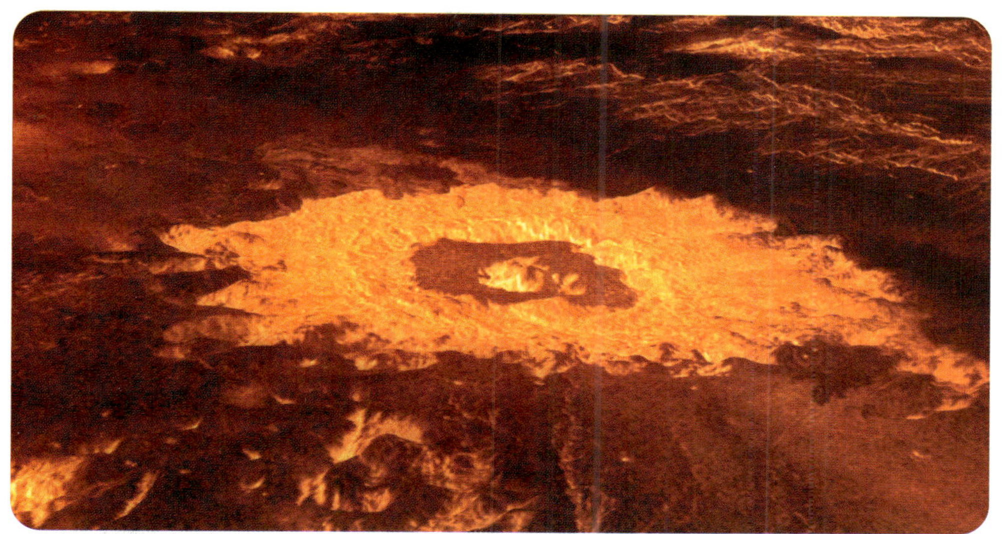

______ is the brightest planet in the solar system.

Planets - Earth and Mars

Earth and Mars are also called inner planets. They are smaller in size as compared to other planets and have a rocky surface. The inner planets are sometimes called rocky planets.

Earth – The Living Planet

Earth is the largest of all rocky planets. It takes about 365 days to travel around the sun. Earth is the only planet in the solar system to support life. The optimum distance from the sun, a favourable atmosphere, and the presence of water make life possible on earth.

Mars – The Red Planet

Mars orbits the sun in about 687 days, which means that a year on Mars is twice as long as a year on Earth. It has rocks and clay rich in iron, which gives it a red colour.

Earth-like Planet

Like Earth, Mars has some of the tallest volcanoes and deepest valleys. Olympus Mons is the tallest mountain on Mars. The surface of the planet also has craters which were made when large objects hit the planet. Even water is present here in the form of ice, frost, fog and clouds.

- Earth rotates on its axis and takes 23 hours, 56 minutes, and 4.09 seconds to complete one orbit.
- Mars has clouds in its atmosphere and ice at its north pole.

Which planet is called as Red Planet?

Planets - Jupiter and Saturn

After the four inner planets, come the outer planets. Jupiter and Saturn are two of the four outer planets. Outer planets are larger than inner planets and are gaseous. They also have rings around them.

Jupiter

Jupiter is the largest planet in the solar system. It is so huge that more than 1300 Earths could fit inside it. It completes one orbit around the sun in about 11.86 years. However, it spins on its axis very fast, as a day on Jupiter is only 9 hours and 55 minutes long.

Storms and Clouds

Jupiter is a huge ball of gases and liquids. The planet has dense red, brown, yellow, and white clouds. These clouds change their colours daily. Powerful winds sweep across the planet.

Saturn

Saturn is the second-largest planet. The planet is made up of materials that are lighter than water. So, if Saturn were placed in a pool, it would float.

The Rings

Saturn is surrounded by a flat layer of thin rings. The layer has seven broad rings and thousands of narrow ringlets. These ringlets are made up of billions of pieces of dust, which could be as small as pebbles or as large as skyscrapers.

- The Great Red Spot on Jupiter is a large hurricane-like storm in the Southern Hemisphere.
- Saturn takes 29.5 years to go around the sun.

Saturn is the largest planet in the solar system. (True or False)

Planets -Uranus and Neptune

Like Jupiter and Saturn, Uranus and Neptune are also called outer planets. Since all the outer planets are made of gases, they are sometimes called gas giants. There is no solid rocky surface to land on on these planets.

Uranus

Uranus is the third-largest planet. It takes 84 years to complete its trip around the sun. Uranus is a very cold and windy planet as it is far away from the Sun. Clouds of bluish-green colour cover the planet. These clouds are made of methane gas. Uranus also has eleven rings made of dark, rock-sized particles.

Neptune

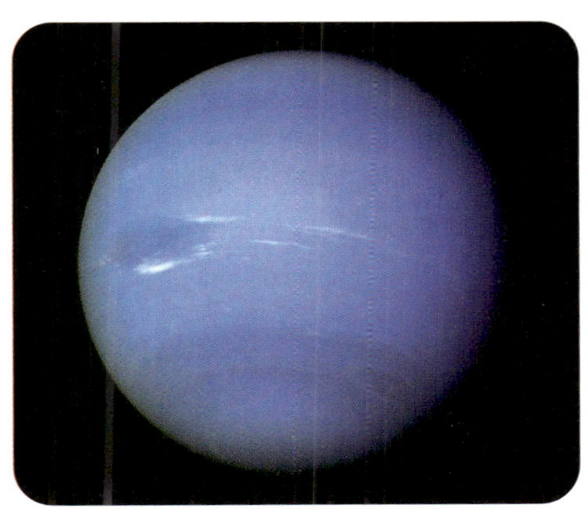

Neptune is last and the farthest planet from the sun. It is so far away that it cannot be seen without a telescope. The planet also has methane gas in abundance which gives the planet its blue color. The planet also has six rings.

Windy Planet

The surface of Neptune has large, dark circles that could be storms. Fast winds blow on it all the time. They can reach speeds of over 2,000 kilometres per hour. Wispy white clouds move across Neptune. According to scientists, there might be scalding hot water present beneath the clouds of the planet.

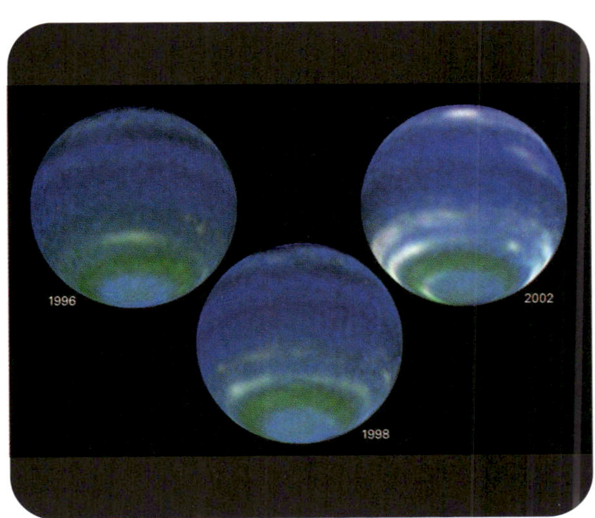

- Neptune takes 165 years to go around the sun.
- For many years, astronomers thought that Uranus was a star.

Uranus and Neptune appear bluish in colour because of presence of _________ in their atmosphere.

Earth's Moon

Moons are natural satellites of planets. Natural satellites are objects that orbit around planets. Moons are smaller than the planets around which they orbit.

Surface of the Moon

The surface of the moon is rocky and has craters, mountains and valleys. The moon has no atmosphere.

Facts

- Neil Armstrong was the first person to walk on the moon on 20th July, 1969.
- A total of 12 astronauts have walked on the moon.

How does it shine?

The moon does not make its own light. It reflects the light coming from the sun. When sunlight hits the surface of the moon, it bounces back to the earth. This is why the moon appears to shine brightly.

Phases of the Moon

The moon revolves around the earth. As it makes its trip around the earth, we see the lit-up part of the moon changing shapes. These different shapes are called phases of the moon. The moon appears to grow from a thin crescent to a full moon and then shrink to a thin crescent again. When the moon appears to be growing in size, it is called waxing. When it appears to be shrinking in size, it is called waning.

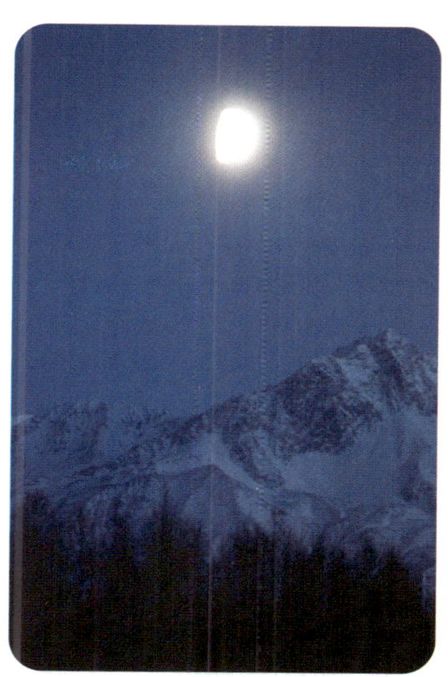

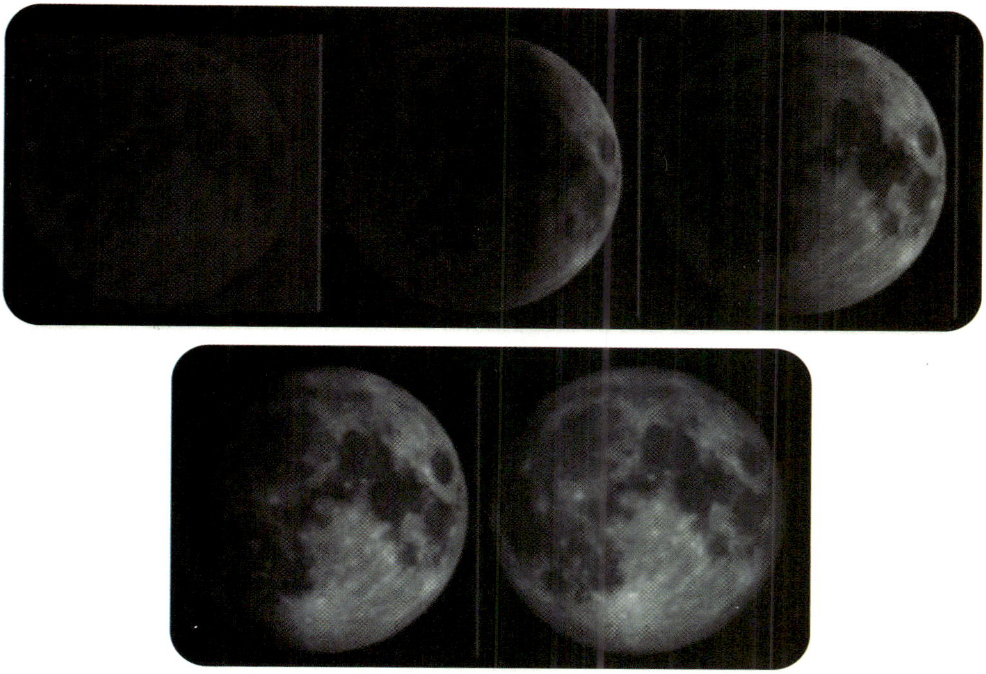

Phases of the Moon

Is there atmosphere on the moon?

Moons of Other Planets

Like Earth, Mars, Jupiter, Saturn, Uranus, and Neptune have moons. Of all these planets, Jupiter has the highest number of moons. The only planets that do have moons are Mercury and Venus.

Saturn's Moons

Saturn has 25 moons that measure at least nine kilometres (about 6 miles) in diameter. Titan is Saturn's largest moon, and it is one of the few satellites in the solar system that has an atmosphere similar to Earth's.

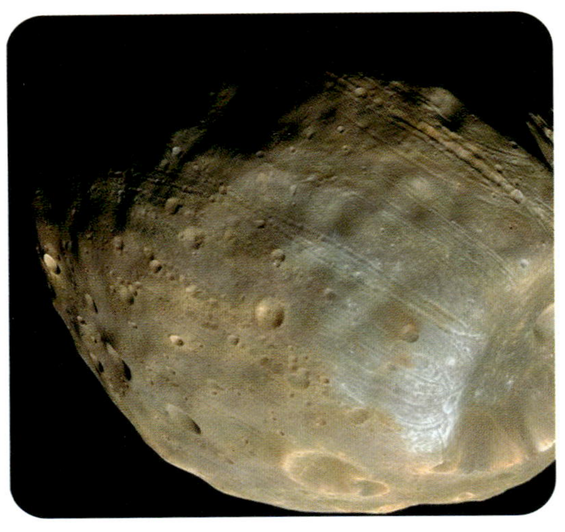

Mars' Moons

Mars is our nearest neighbour in the solar system and has two moons—Phobos and Deimos. They are not spherical like most moons but are uneven and look more like potatoes.

Jupiter's Moons

Jupiter has between 80 to 95 moons, four of which are the largest of the solar system. The four largest moons are—Io, Europa, Ganymede and Callisto.

Facts

- Ariel is the brightest moon of Uranus.
- Neptune has thirteen known moons.
- Many moons of Uranus are named after the characters of Shakespeare's plays.

Uranus' Moons

Uranus has 27 known moons. Scientists think that there may be more undiscovered moons. Out of 27 moons, five are very large, and the rest are small. The five large moons are named Ariel, Umbriel, Titania, Oberon, and Miranda. Of all the moons, Titania is the largest.

How many moons does Jupiter have?

Comet

Comets are small, icy bodies that orbit around the sun. Comets are the icy remains of rocks, gases, and dust. Most comets cannot be seen with the naked eye. Some comets, however, become visible as they pass close to the sun, appearing as a streak of bright light.

Parts of a Comet

The head of a comet is a solid core made of icy dust and rock particles. It is surrounded by a cloudy atmosphere known as the coma and has one or two tails. The dust and gas of the coma and the tails reflect sunlight, which allows us to see the comet from Earth.

- The tail of a comet always points away from the sun.
- The earliest comet was seen in 1059 BC in China.

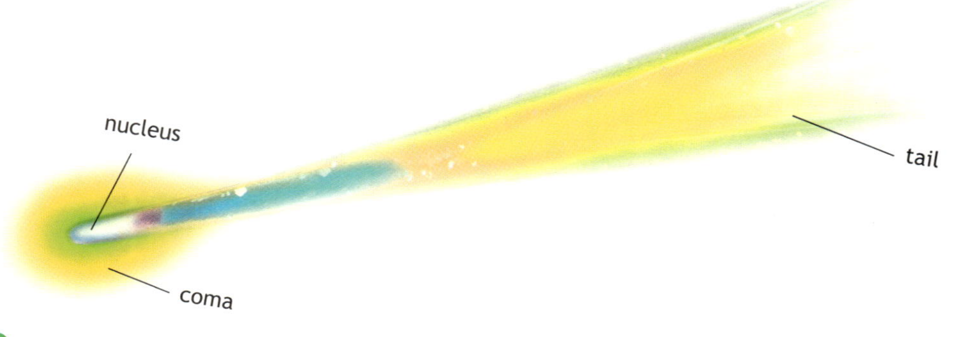

Birth of Comets

Comet comes from a Latin word meaning long-haired. Astronomers believe that most of the comets come from two regions: the Kuiper Belt and the Oort Cloud. The Kuiper Belt is a space of icy remains between Neptune and Pluto. The Oort Cloud is a circular covering that surrounds the solar system.

Types of Comets

Comets can be short-period comets or long-period comets. Their type is determined by how much time it takes to complete an orbit around the sun. Short-period comets come from the Kuiper Belt and take less than 200 years to complete one orbit. Long-period comets come from the Oort Cloud and take more than 200 years to complete one orbit.

? Long period comets come from ______.

Asteroids and Meteors

Asteroids are small rocky bodies that move around the sun. Asteroids can be as small as a pebble or as large as a few hundred miles in diameter. Meteors are bright streaks of light falling on earth. They appear when metal or stony matter burns up when entering the earth's atmosphere.

Asteroid Belt

The Asteroid Belt, also known as the Main Belt, is a region between the orbits of Mars and Jupiter. The region is more than 150 million kilometres (92 million miles) wide and contains thousands of asteroids. Until now, astronomers have been able to identify and number roughly one million asteroids asteroids.

Asteroid vs Comet

Asteroids are different from comets only in their composition. Asteroids are made up of metals and rocky materials, while comets are made up of ice, dust and rocky materials. Asteroids were formed as a result of cosmic explosions, which happened about 4.6 billion years ago.

Meteoroids and Meteors

Meteoroids are metal-like or stone-like debris present in space. When meteoroids enter the earth's atmosphere, they heat up and begin to glow. They are known as meteors. Meteors appear as a streak of light in the sky; many call them shooting stars or falling stars. Most of the meteors burn up before reaching the earth. However, any meteor that reaches the surface of the earth is called a meteorite.

- Every 50 to 100 million years, the earth is hit by a 10-kilometre (about 6-mile) large asteroid.
- The largest asteroid crater is in Vredefort, South Africa. It is 300 kilometres (about 186 miles) in diameter.
- Asteroids can also have their own moons.

Where is the largest asteroid crater?

Black Holes and Quasars

A black hole is a dark, dense region of space with immense gravity. Scientists believe that there is a supermassive black hole at the centre of each galaxy. Quasars are very bright, star-like objects present at the end of the universe. They give off a lot of energy and are a trillion times brighter than the sun.

Sagittarius A*

Sagittarius A* (Sgr A*) is the supermassive black hole at the Galactic Centre of the Milky Way. Scientists believe that the black hole is about four million times more massive than the mass of the Sun.

Quasars

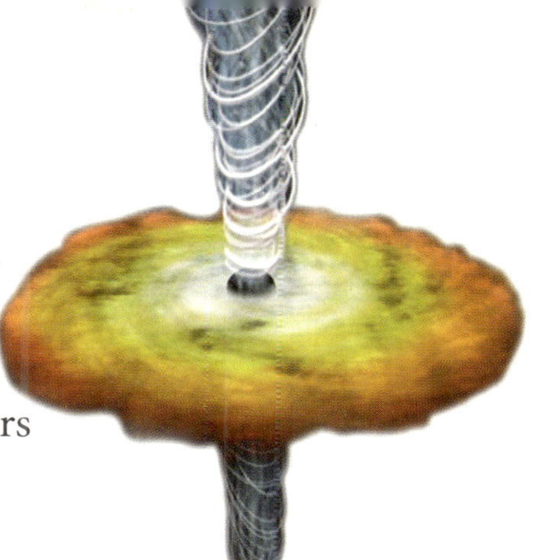

Quasars are billions of light years away from the earth. They get their energy from massive black holes, which are at the centre of the quasar's galaxy. Quasars use their energy to shine brightly.

Facts

- The Sun is too small to become a black hole.
- Black holes are detected by the objects near them.
- Quasars are so bright that they outshine nearby stars.

How are black holes formed?

Black holes are formed when massive stars run out of nuclear fuel and get crushed by their own gravitational force. Unable to support their own weight, their core collapses, which forms a black hole.

What is a quasar?

Spaces Probes

Space probes are flights sent into space to collect information and pictures about the universe. They are usually sent to planets, moons, comets, and asteroids. Some of these are controlled by humans, while most of them are controlled directly by computers.

Luna 1

Luna 1 was the first successful space probe. It was launched towards the moon in 1959. Luna 1 passed within 6,000 kilometres (about 3,728 miles) of the Moon's surface after 34 hours of space travel. After passing by the moon, it went into orbit around the sun, between the orbits of Earth and Mars.

Facts

- Valentina Tereshkova was the first woman to travel into space.
- Voyager 1 is the most distant spacecraft from Earth.

Mariner 2

Mariner 2 was the first successful space probe to reach another planet in the solar system. It was sent to Venus on August 26, 1962, and travelled about 34,773 kilometres (about 21,607 miles). Mariner 2 observed that Venus has cool clouds and an extremely hot surface.

Space Probe Journeys

Space probes may orbit a planet or a moon. They may also land on a surface to study it. They may remain there or bring data and information back to earth. Most of them send data from space by radio with the help of a process known as telemetry.

Name the first successful space probe to reach another planet.

Astronomers

Astronomy is the scientific study of the universe. Scientists who study astronomy are called astronomers. Astronomers use telescopes to study the universe. They study celestial objects such as planets, comets, asteroids, meteors, stars, and galaxies. They also study celestial events, such as solar and lunar eclipses.

Giovanni Domenico Cassini

Giovanni Domenico Cassini was an Italian-born French astronomer. He observed a large gap between the multiple rings of Saturn. This gap was named the Cassini Division after him.

Facts

- The Cassini-Huygens spacecraft was built with the help of 17 nations and three space agencies.
- The Hubble Space Telescope is named after the American astronomer, Edwin Hubble.

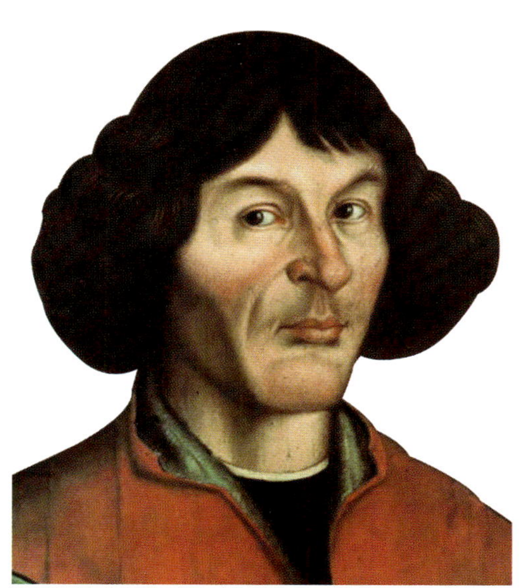

Nicolaus Copernicus

Copernicus was the founder of modern astronomy. He discovered that the earth was not at the centre of the solar system. He concluded that the earth and other planets moved around the sun in orbits and that the sun was at the centre of the solar system.

Galileo Galilei

Galileo Galilei was an Italian astronomer and mathematician. He was the first to use telescopes for the study of astronomy. He was the first to discover that the moon has mountains and valleys like the earth. Galileo also discovered the four moons of Jupiter.

Who discovered that the earth was not at the centre of the solar system?

Glossary

Atmosphere: gases enveloping the earth or any other planet

Axis: a real or imaginary straight line on which an object rotates

Celestial: related to space

Collapse: to fall into pieces, after a breakdown

Collide: to crash into one another

Constellation: a group of stars forming patterns in the sky

Cosmic: anything related to the universe as a whole

Diffuse: when something is spread out in every direction

Emission: a gas-like substance that goes into the air or the act of sending out gases into the air

Equator: an imaginary line on earth that divides the earth into the northern and southern hemispheres

Explosion: when something bursts or blows out

Giant: huge

Gravity: a force that attracts everything towards itself

Halt: a stop in a movement or process

Light-year: a unit for measuring distance in space that is calculated by the distance that light travels in a year

Mystery: something that a person cannot understand and explain

Mythological: a set of beliefs held by many people that are not true

Particle: small and tiny pieces of anything

Pebble: a small and smooth stone

Robotic rover: a vehicle that moves around the planets through computer signals

Spacecraft: a vehicle built to travel in space

Spherical: having the shape of a sphere or a ball

Spiral: coiling around a fixed line

Telescope: an instrument that makes faraway things look closer

Volcano: a mountain from which lava, hot gases, rocks, and sand ash come out with force and an explosion

Answers

Page No. 51	Yes
Page No. 53	Spiral
Page No. 55	Constellation of Draco
Page No. 57	100,000 light-years
Page No. 59	A dwarf planet
Page No. 61	4.6 billion years
Page No. 63	Supernovae
Page No. 65	Venus
Page No. 67	Mars
Page No. 69	False
Page No. 71	Methane gas
Page No. 73	No
Page No. 75	63
Page No. 77	Oort cloud
Page No. 79	Vredefort, South Africa
Page No. 81	Bright star-like object
Page No. 83	Mariner 2
Page No. 85	On February 19, 1473